A Step In Time

A Kid's Guide To Ephesus, Turkey

Photography By John D. Weigand
Poetry By Penelope Dyan

Bellissima Publishing, LLC
Jamul, California
www.bellissimapublishing.com

copyright © 2011 by Penny D. Weigand and John D. Weigand

All rights reserved. No part of this book may be reproduced or transmitted in any form or by any means, electronic or mechanical, including photocopying, recording, or by any other means, or by any information or storage retrieval system, without permission from the publisher.

ISBN 978-1-935630-57-9

First Edition

TIME IS ETERNAL.

A Step In Time
Bellissima Publishing, LLC

INTRODUCTION

Ephesus, Turkey is an exciting place to visit, full of history and culture and more facts than you could ever possibly keep inside your head, so the best thing to do when you go to this place is to simply soak it in, relax and take a step back in time as you explore this part of Turkey, which is actually a part of Asia. The Turks will tell you that people who are from this part of Turkey in Asia were the first settlers of America, the first Native Americans. They will tell you that it was their ancestors who crossed the Bering Strait during the ice age, and that their people are Nomadic and to them at that time, it made perfect sense. The problem was the ice that made up the bridge to America melted, and they could not come home. Looking at the traditional rugs (as you will see in this book) lend credence to this theory, because the art of the weave and the manner of the weaving, dying and creation of the rugs of the Navajo and these Nomadic Turks (today) look almost exactly the same.

Travel through this book's pages and take a glimpse at Izmir Turkey with award winning writer, attorney and former teacher, Penelope Dyan and master photographer John D. Weeigand, and behold the magic of Turkey!

A Step In Time
Bellissima Publishing, LLC

A Step In Time
A Kid's Guide To Ephesus, Turkey

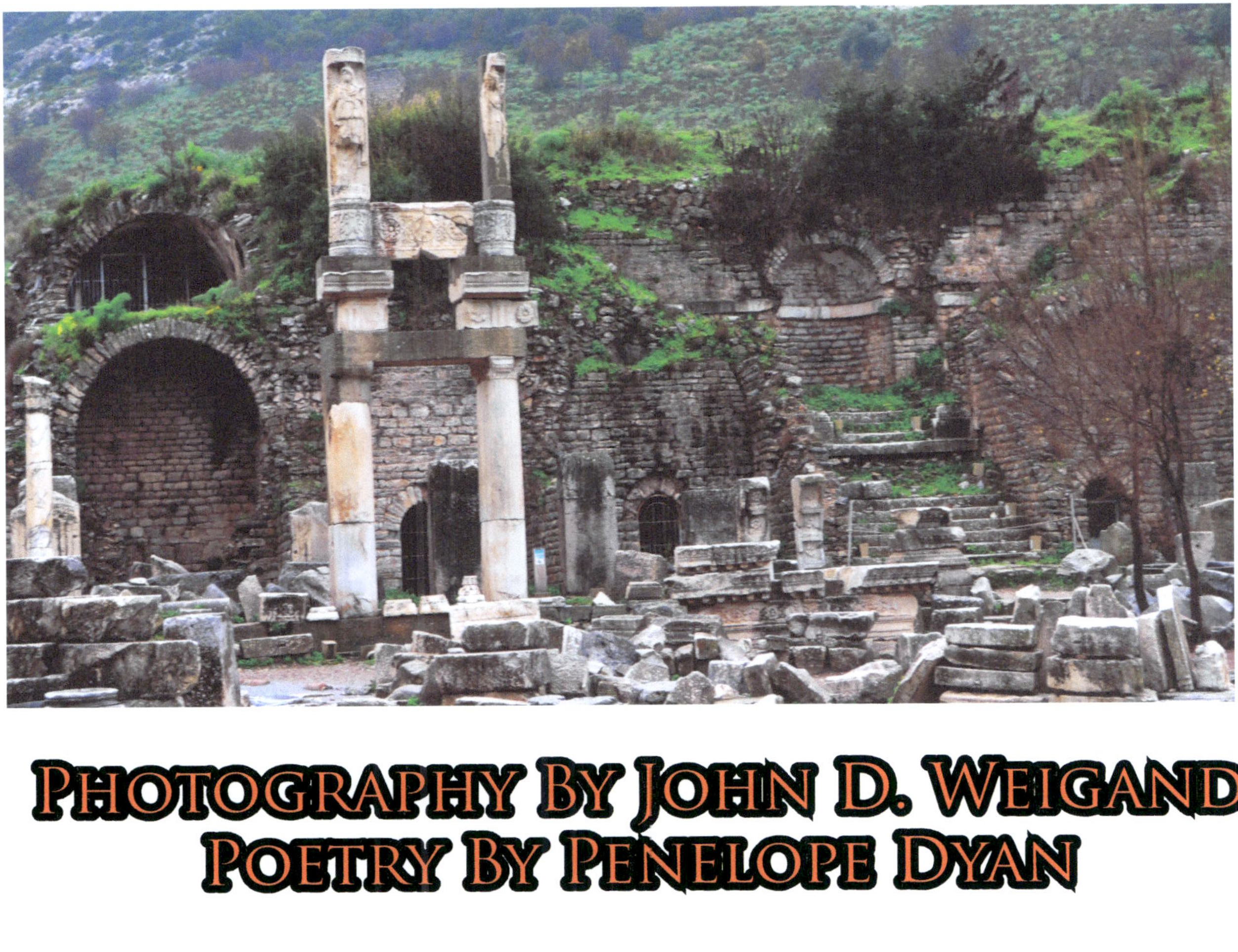

Photography By John D. Weigand
Poetry By Penelope Dyan

In Ephesus there is a place where the people make rugs at an extraordinary pace!

It is the nomadic people who make rugs in this store...

They make simply beautiful rugs!
They make rugs galore!

Here a woman is making beautiful silk thread!
But you CAN purchase a WOOL rug instead.

They dye the wool, cotton and silk yarns
with roots, herbs, leaves and grass---
And they make a product
that is meant to last!

A woman weaves a rug sitting at a loom. It is made all by hand, so it won't be done soon.

Then you go to ANCIENT Ephesus, and you see the angel Nike... as clear as can be.
And I have to wonder... if perhaps you, have the symbol of Nike upon your little shoe?

In Ancient Ephesus Roman columns you will find,
made of different stone of many a kind.
They held up canopies that covered the street,
that kept dry the chariots and the horses' feet.

This was once the Rodeo Drive of these very
ancient Roman times.
You could buy clothes here and jewelry here
and things of many different kinds.
And I wonder... and don't you wonder too?
If upon THEIR feet, they wore a Nike shoe?

This is a bathroom just for men,
where they had to go and sit.
(And you know EXACTLY when!)
But the women ALL had to go home,
because there was NO public bathroom
(FOR THEM) made of stone.
And they even had an orchestra
right inside of there.
And the men discussed politics and business,
and as to THIS I swear!

Here are some stairs that you can climb,
to explore these places so ancient and sublime!
And you may even see a very small mouse,
ancestors of mice who once lived in this house.
And THIS is probably why there are also cats,
to hunt and eat the Ephesus' mice and rats.
But please do not worry; it is not Mickey Mouse,
who will be roaming about THIS ancient house.

Here is a monument with a Medusa of its own,
So that you would bow to HADRIAN,
and NOT look up and turn to stone!

And at last you see the library, tall and proud.
Even absent all its books, it still draws a crowd.

As you LEAVE the ancient city you can shop.
You can buy Genie shoes, a scarf or spinning top.
And as you look around each store,
You will find there is one thing more....

There are lots and lots of evil eyes,
and you will purchase one if you are wise.
Because these evil eyes actually
chase evil AWAY!
They represent good luck in the
old TURKISH way!
You will see many things here!
And you WILL have fun,
even if it's raining
and even IF there is NO sun!
Because there is one thing HERE
that WILL last and last!
AND that ONE thing is the ANCIENT past.
And no matter WHERE you go,
and no matter WHERE the place,
You will find there is NOTHING more fantastic
than the AMAZING human race.

"Each of us will leave an imprint in the sand, upon the earth, and upon the land. This is how it has to be. Because this is our destiny."

Penelope Dyan

www.ingramcontent.com/pod-product-compliance
Ingram Content Group UK Ltd.
Pitfield, Milton Keynes, MK11 3LW, UK
UKHW060137240426
12048UKWH00002B/70